THE CYDER-MAKER'S INSTRUCTOR, SWEET-MAKER'S ASSISTANT, AND VICTUALLER'S AND HOUSEKEEPER'S DIRECTOR

THE CYDER-MAKER'S INSTRUCTOR, SWEET-MAKER'S ASSISTANT, AND VICTUALLER'S AND HOUSEKEEPER'S DIRECTOR

THOMAS CHAPMAN

ISBN: 978-93-89614-27-5

Published: 1762

LECTOR HOUSE LLP
E-MAIL: lectorpublishing@gmail.com

THE CYDER-MAKER'S INSTRUCTOR, SWEET-MAKER'S ASSISTANT, AND VICTUALLER'S AND HOUSEKEEPER'S DIRECTOR.

IN THREE PARTS.

* * * * *

PART I.

Directs the grower to make his cyder in the manner foreign wines are made; to preserve its body and flavour; to lay on a colour, and to cure all its disorders, whether bad flavour'd, prick'd, oily, or ropy.

PART II.

Instructs the trader or housekeeper to make raisin-wines, at a small Expence, little (if any thing) inferior to foreign wines in strength or flavour; to cure their disorders; to lay on them new bodies, colour, &c.

PART III.

Directs the brewer to fine his beer and ale in a short time, and to cure them if prick'd or ropy.

To which is added, A Method to make yest to ferment beer, as well as common yest, when that is not to be had.

All actually deduced from the *author's* experience.

BY

THOMAS CHAPMAN, WINE-COOPER.

MDCCLXII.

THE PREFACE.

It may be thought necessary, in compliance with custom, that I should say something by way of PREFACE. If the reader would be informed what my reasons were for appearing in print, I shall candidly acknowledge, that the great prospect of a considerable advantage to myself was indeed the strongest persuasive; but I can with equal truth affirm, that it affords me no small pleasure to think I am doing my country at the same time a very great piece of service; and doubt not but that, as many will soon experience it, my labour will be thankfully received and acknowledged.

Discoveries and Improvements ought not to be concealed; the public good calls loudly for them; but then, in return for the great advantage the public receives from them, the author of any such discovery may with the greatest justice claim an adequate reward.

PREFACE

The following Receipts and Directions are not collected from books, nor interspersed with old women's nostrums; but they are, in very truth, the result of my own LONG EXPERIENCE in trade, founded on chemical principles, which are principles of never-erring nature.

Perhaps I had never thought of this Method of communicating my little knowledge, had it not been for many gentlemen in the counties of *Gloucester, Hereford, Worcester,* &c. for whom I have done a great deal of business, in the cyder-way particularly; and who have often express'd their desire of seeing my directions for the management of cyders, &c. made public.

And no doubt such a thing was wanting; for it's hardly credible how much liquors of almost every kind is spoiled by mismanagement. Few people know the nature of fermentation, without which no vinous spirit can be produced; nor any liquor be rendered fine and potible.

Fermentation separates the particles of bodies, and from liquids throws off the gross parts from the finer, which, without it, could not be effected. There is what is called a *fret,* which is only a partial fermentation, that nature is strong enough in some liquors to bring on, without the assistance of art; but this *fret,* or partial fermentation, is never strong enough to discharge the liquor of its foul parts; and if they should ever happen to subside, the least alteration in weather, as well as a hundred other accidents, will occasion their commixing, and render the liquor almost, or altogether as foul as ever; to prevent which we call in the assistance of art, and which our method will effectually prevent.

In brewing beer, yest is apply'd to it, in order to ferment it, without which it would never be beer. This opens the body of the liquor, and renders it spirity and fine.

The reason that cyder is not often fine, is owing to its not being fermented. After it is got into the hogshead, the generality of people think they have acquitted themselves very well, and done all the necessary business, except racking it. But I can assure them, the more any liquor is rack'd, the more it is weaken'd. By often racking, it loseth its body, and so becomes acid for want of strength to support it.

Another gross error many people are guilty of, in keeping the bungs out of the casks. Nothing is more pernicious to fermented liquors, than their being exposed to the open air, whereby they lose their strength and flavour. Take a bottle of wine, draw the cork, and let it stand exposed to the open air for twenty-four hours only, and you will then find it dead, flat, and insipid; for the spirit is volatile, and has been carried off by the air, and what remains is the gross, elementary part chiefly. A cyder-cask should never be kept open more than fourteen or fifteen days, that is, 'till the ferment is stopt; but so contrary is the practice, that I have known them very commonly kept open three or four months. It hath been objected to me by cyder and sweet-makers, that stopping up the cask so soon will endanger the head being blown out or bursted; but their fears are groundless, provided the ferment is stopt. The bottoms are quite confined, and it is impossible they should rise, unless a forcing be added to raise them.

The best time for bottling your cyder, is in the winter, or cool weather, when it is *down*, otherwise you will hazard breaking most of the bottles. The best method of keeping it, is to put it up in dry saw-dust, which will keep it in a due temperature of heat, without the colour's subsiding, unless you have laid a high colour on it, which, by long keeping, will subside in the same manner port-wine doth in bottles. For 'tis impossible to set a colour on cyder so strong, as to have it stand the bottle more than twelve or eighteen months, at farthest. The natural colour will change but little in a much longer time.

What I have said of the sweet-making-business, (which I have been constantly concerned in for more than twenty years) is principally relating to fermentation; for it is in all kinds of made-wines the chief thing to be observed. I shall just take notice here of one or two things, by way of caution.

If your fruit be candied, the best way to clean them is by bagging, and then you may easily take the stems from them.

It is very seldom that the fruit is all of the same goodness, I would therefore recommend, that the best fruit be made separate from the ordinary, it being easy, and much more prudent, to mix the liquors to your palate, than to run the hazard of making the good fruit with the bad, a small quantity of which will sometimes spoil the flavour of the liquor, and turn it acid.

As to the method of brewing malt-liquors, I shall only here observe, that the practice of boiling the wort so long as is often done, is very injudicious. Five minutes is long enough: a longer time serves only to evaporate the spirit, without having any good effect.

Under the head of malt-liquor, I have confined myself to giving proper instructions for curing their disorders, such as fining 'em, *&c.* which must be of great use to victuallers as well as private families, who, by reason of the badness of malt, mismanagement, bad weather, or other accidents, have frequently quantities by them, which for want of knowing how to cure, lie useless, and are sometimes thrown away.

In the course of these receipts, I have endeavoured to lay down every thing as plain as possible, preferring, in these cases, plainness to elegance, even tho' I were capable of it, which indeed I have no pretensions to.

Before I take leave of my reader, I must admonish him, that if my directions are not observed punctually, I will not be answerable for his success; for he may be assured, in matters of this kind, a great deal depends upon what many people think trifling, and of no consequence whether done or not. But on the other hand, if he will take care to observe them exactly, I am sure they will fully answer his expectations. So shall he not repent laying out his money on this *little*, but not the least *valuable*, book; nor will my reputation suffer in having penn'd it for his use; which is the earnest wish of

His humble Servant,
T.C.

CONTENTS

PART I.

THE CYDER-MAKER'S INSTRUCTOR.

Let your fruit be as near the same ripeness as possible, otherwise the juice will not agree in fermenting. When they are properly sweated, grind and press them; and as soon as you have filled a cask, if a hogshead, which is one hundred and ten gallons, ferment it as follows; and if less, proportion the ingredients to your quantity.

A FERMENT FOR CYDER.

To one hogshead of cyder, take three pints of solid yest, the mildest you can get; if rough, wash it in warm water, and let it stand 'till it is cold. Pour the water from it, and put it in a pail or can; put to it as much jalap as will lay on a six-pence, beat them well together with a whisk, then apply some of the cyder to it by degrees 'till your can is full. Put it all to the cyder, and stir it well together. When the ferment comes on, you must clean the bung-holes every morning with your finger, and keep filling the vessel up. The ferment for the first five or six days will be black and stiff; let it stand till it ferments white and kind, which it will do in fourteen or fifteen days; at that time stop the ferment, otherwise it will impair its strength.

TO STOP THE FERMENT.

In stopping this ferment, which is a very strong one, you must first rack it into a clean cask, and when pretty near full, put to it three pounds of course, red, scowering sand, and stir it well together with a strong stick, and fill it within a gallon of being full; let it stand five or six hours, then pour on it as softly as you can a gallon of English spirit, and bung it up close; but leave out the vent-peg a day or two. At that time just put it in the hole and close it by degrees till you have got it close. Let it lay in that state at least a year, and if very strong cyder, such as stire, the longer you keep it the better it will be in the body; and when you pierce it, if not bright, force it in the following manner.

A FORCING FOR CYDER.

Take a gallon of perry or stale beer, put to it one ounce of isinglass, beat well and cut or pull'd to small pieces; put it to the perry or beer, and let it steep three or four days. Keep whisking it together, or else the glass will stick to the bottom, and have no effect on the liquor. When it comes to a stiff jelly, beat it well in your can with a whisk, and mix some of the cyder with it, 'till you have made the gallon four; then put two pounds of brick rubbings to it, and stir it together with two gallons of cyder more added to it, and apply to the hogshead; stir it well with your paddle, and shive it up close. The next day give it vent, and you will find it fine and bright. If you force perry, cut your isinglass with cyder or stale beer, for no liquor will force its own body.

TO CURE ACID CYDER.

It is always to be observ'd, that even weak *alkali*'s cure the strongest acid, such, for instance, as calcin'd chalk, calcin'd oyster or scallop-shells, calcin'd egg-shells, alabaster, &c. But if a hogshead can soon be drank, use a stronger *alkali*, such as salt of tartar, salt of wormwood; but in using them, you must always preserve their colour with *lac*, or else the *alkali* will turn the liquor black, and keep it foul.

To one hogshead, take two gallons of *lac*, and put to it one ounce and a half of isinglass beat well and pulled small; boil them together for five or six minutes; drain it, and when a stiff jelly, break it with a whisk, and mix about a gallon of the cyder with it; then put three pounds of calcin'd chalk, and two pounds of calcined oyster-shells to it, whisk it well together with four gallons more of the cyder, and apply it to the hogshead. Stir it well, and it will immediately discharge the acid part out at the bung. Let it stand one hour, then bung it close for five or six days; rack it from the bottom into a clean hogshead, and apply one quart of forcing to it. If you use a strong *alkali*, put to the *lac* four ounces of salt of tartar, or salt of wormwood; but the former is best, as it hath not the bitter taste in it which the wormwood has.

Note, Lac *is milk, but the cream must be skimm'd off it for use.*

TO CURE OILY CYDER.

The reason that cyder is sometimes oily, is owing to the fruit not being sorted alike; for the juice of fruit that is not ripe will seldom mix with ripe juice in fermentation. The acid part of one will predominate over the other, and throw the oily particles from it, which separation gives the liquor a disagreeable, foul taste; to remedy which you must treat it in the following manner, which will cause the oily parts to swim at top, and then you may rack the liquor from its bottom and oil.

To a hogshead, take an ounce of salt of tartar, and two ounces of half sweet spirit of nitre, mix them in a gallon of *lac*, and whisk them well together; apply it to the hogshead, bung it up, and let it stand ten or fifteen days; then put a cock within two inches of the bottom of the hogshead, and rack it.

Observe when it runs low, to look to the cock, lest any of the oily part should come, which will be all on the top, and will not run out till after the good liquor is drawn off.

Put to the clean a quart of forcing, to raise it, and bung it close.

Note, When you take out the oil and bottom, your cask must be well fired, otherwise it will spoil all the liquor that shall be afterwards put into it.

FOR ROPY CYDER.

The following remedy for ropy cyder must be proportion'd with judgment to the degree of the disorder in the liquor. If the rope be stiff and stringy, you must use a larger quantity of the ingredients.

If a hogshead be quite stiff and stringy, work it at least an hour with your paddle, then put to it six pounds of common allum, ground to a fine powder; work it for half an hour after, and bung it up close. This in a week will cut the rope and bring it to a fine, thin, fluid state. Then rack it into a clean hogshead, and put to it one quart of forcing; stir them well in the hogshead and bung it close up. If but a thin rope, use a less quantity of the allum, and work it the same way.

CYDERS BAD FLAVOUR'D.

Some cyders in keeping are apt to get reasty, thro' the ill quality of the fruit; and sometimes thro' the badness of the cask will get musty, or fusty.

To remedy these evils, you must throw it in ferment, if its body is strong, with yest and jalap, and let it ferment three or four days; which will throw off the greatest part of the taste; then stop the ferment. If a hogshead, put to it one pound of sweet spirit of nitre, and bung it up close. This will cure the bad flavour if any left, and likewise keep it from growing flat.

TO COLOUR CYDER.

In many places, particularly where the soil is light, and the orchard lays rising, the juice of the fruit is nearly white, and tho' the cyder may be strong, it doth not appear to be so, by reason of its colour, which always prejudices the buyer against it.

Many people spoil a great deal of good cyder by boiling and mixing melasses with it, to give it a colour; which not only gives it a bad red colour, but makes it muddy, as well as bad tasted. Others, again, will boil a large quantity of brown sugar and mix with it, which gives it a colour indeed, tho' a light one; when two pounds of good sugar, properly used, is sufficient to colour ten hogsheads, as follows:

Take two pounds of powder sugar, the whiter the sugar the farther it will go, and the better the colour will be. Put it in an iron pot or ladle; set it over the fire, and let it burn 'till it is black and bitter; then put two quarts of boiling hot water to it; keep stirring it about, and boil it a quarter of an hour after you have put the water to it. Take it off the fire, and let it stand 'till it is cold; then bottle it for use.

Half a pint of this will colour a hogshead. Put to each half pint, when you use it, a quarter of an ounce of allum ground, to set the colour.

PART II.

THE SWEET-MAKER'S ASSISTANT.

OF RAISIN WINES.

These wines are made of various kinds of fruit; of *Malaga's, Belvederes, Smyrna's, Raisins of the Sun*, &c. But the fruit that produces the best wines is black *Smyrna's*, their juice being the strongest, and the fruit clearest from stalks: for the stalks in *Malaga's* and *Belvideres* are apt to give the wine a bad flavour, and will always throw an acid on it; for the stalks of all fruits are acid; but the stalks of *Smyrna's* are so trifling, that after rubbing the fruit between your hands, they will easily sift out. Wine made from this fruit is the colour of Madeira, and has very much the flavour of it. Malaga is the colour and flavour of foreign malaga, but nothing near so strong. Wine made from belvideres is strong and very sweet; and after keeping it four or five years is very little inferior to old mountain.

In order to succeed in making these wines, you ought never to set your steeps in hot weather, because the heat will put the fruit in a fret which will injure its fermenting kindly. The best time for making is in January or February. Set your steeps in the coldest part of the cellar, still remembering to keep them from the frost.

To every gallon of water put five pounds of fruit, if good; if but indifferent, put six pounds, into the steep. Keep stirring them three or four times a day, and let them continue in the steep till the fruit begins to burst, and the stones swim on the top; which will be in about fourteen or fifteen days. Then strain the liquor from the fruit, and press the fruit very dry, mixing the pressings with the rest of the liquor, and put all together into a cask, and ferment it in the following manner.

To every pipe of wine take two quarts of solid ale yest and one ounce of jalap, put them into a can, and into them pour a gallon of the new wine first made hot, whisk them well together, and apply to the pipe, stirring all together very well. If your cask be less than a pipe, proportion your yest and jalap accordingly. When the ferment comes on, you must keep the bung-hole clean, and let the vessel be filled up three or four times a day. Let it ferment ten or twelve days, or till it works clean and white. Then take it off its bottom, which will be very considerable, and put it into a clean cask. You may filter the bottom thro' a linen rag and put to the wine. Lay some heavy weight over the bung, and let it stand a day. Then lay on the top of the wine five gallons of melasses-spirit, and bung it up close. Leave out the vent peg a day or two; then drop it in the hole, and close it by degrees 'till you have made it quite close.

Let it lay in this state for six months, at that time rack it from its bottom into a clean pipe, and you'll find it tolerably fine. Then put to it one quart of *forcing*, and bung it up. Let it lay 'till within a month of your wanting it; for the longer it lays the better it will be in body. Then rack it for the last time (always observing you touch no bottoms) and put three pints of *forcing* to it. Stir it well with your paddle, and bung it up. The bottoms you may run thro' a linen rag as before, and mix with that in the pipe. You may pierce the wine in six or seven days, and you will find it quite fine and bright.

TO FORCE RAISIN WINES.

For one pipe, take two quarts of good cyder; put half an ounce of ground allum to it, and one ounce of isinglass pulled to small pieces. Beat them well in your can three or four times a day, and let the mixture stand till it becomes a stiff jelly; then break it with your whisk, and add to it two pounds of white sand or stone dust. Then break it up gradually with some of the wine, 'till you have made the two quarts two gallons, stir it well together, and apply to the pipe, and bung up close.

The sand will carry down with it all the small particles with the isinglass misses, and likewise confine the bottom so as to prevent it from rising. But if you make your wine stronger by allowing a larger quantity of fruit to the gallon, this *forcing* will not do; for all *forcings* must be stronger than the body forc'd, or else the foul parts will not fall; therefore such wines must be forced with *English stum*, a quart of which is sufficient for a pipe, one pound of alabaster being beat in with it and apply'd as above.

ENGLISH STUM.

Take a five gallon cask that has been well soaked in water, set it to drain; then take a pound of roll brimstone and melt in a ladle; put as many rags to it as will suck up the melted brimstone. Burn half those rags in the cask, covering the bung-hole so much as that it may have just air enough to keep it burning. When burnt out put three gallons of very strong cyder, and one ounce of common allum (pounded and mixt with the cyder) into the cask. Keep rolling the cask about five or six times a day for two days. Then take out the bung, and hang the remainder of the rags on a wire in the cask, as near the cyder as possible, and set them on fire as before. When burnt out, bung the cask close and roll it well about three or four times a day for two days; then let it stand seven or eight days, and this liquor will be so strong as to affect your eyes by looking at it.

When you force a pipe, take one quart of this liquid, put half an ounce of isinglass to it beat and pulled to small pieces. Whisk it together, and it will dissolve in four or five hours. Break the jelly with your whisk, and put one pound of alabaster to it, then dilute it with some of the wine, put it in the pipe, bung it close, and in a day it will be fine and bright.

TO CURE ACID RAISIN WINES.

The following ingredients must be proportioned to the degree of acidity; if but small, you must use the less, if a stronger acid a larger quantity. It must likewise be proportioned to the quantity of wine as well as to the degree of acidity.

Observe that your cask be nearly full before you apply the ingredients; which will have this good effect, the acid part of the wine will rise to the top immediately, and issue out at the bung-hole. But if the cask be not full, the part that should fly off will still continue in the cask, and weaken the body of the wine. If your cask be full, it will be fit to have a body laid on it, in three or four days time.

I shall here proportion the ingredients for a pipe, supposing it quite acid, so as but just recoverable.

Take two gallons of lac, and two ounces of isinglass, boil them a quarter of an hour; strain the liquor, and let it stand 'till it is cold; then break it well with your whisk, and put four pounds of alabaster and three pounds of whiting to it. Stir them well together, and add one ounce of salt of tartar to the whole. Mix by degrees some of the wine with it, so as to dilute it to a thin liquor. Apply this to the cask, and stir it well with your paddle. This will immediately discharge the acid part from it, as was said before.

When it is off and quite down, bung it up for three days, then rack it, and you'll find part of its body gone off by the strong fermentation. To remedy this, you must lay a fresh body on it in proportion to the degree to which it hath been lower'd by the above process; always having special care not to alter flavour. And this must be done with clarified sugar; for no fluid body will agree with it but what will make it thinner, or confer its own taste; therefore the following is the best manner.

TO LAY A FRESH BODY ON THE WINES.

Take three quarters of a hundred of brown sugar, and put into your copper, then put a gallon of lime water to it, to keep it from burning. Keep stirring it about 'till it boils; then take three eggs and mash all together with the Shells, which put to the sugar. Stir it about, and as the scum or filth arise take it off. When quite clean put it into your can, and let it stand 'till it is cold before you use it. Then break it with the whisk by degrees, with about ten gallons of the wine, and apply it to the pipe. Work it with your paddle for half an hour; then put one quart of *stum forcing* to it, which will unite their bodies, and likewise make it fine and bright. You must keep it bung'd very close.

TO CURE RAISIN WINES THAT ARE CLOUDY.

These wines, if they take a chill, are affected in the same manner with Port-wines. Like them they will be cloudy, and will have a floating lee in them, which by shaking in a glass will rise in clouds.

If any thing be apply'd to it cold, it will strike a greater chill upon it, and change its true colour to a pale or deep blue one; to prevent which, and take off the chill, you must,

For a Pipe,

Take one gallon of lac and one ounce of isinglass broke in small pieces, three pounds of alabaster, two ounces of sweet spirit of nitre; boil them together for five or six minutes; Stir them and apply to the pipe as hot as possible. Stir it well in the pipe with your paddle, and in about two hours after, bung it close up. Let it lay five or six days, and you'll find it quite fine and bright.

This will make it a little flat, to remedy which you must rack it clean from it's bottoms, and throw a quart of *stum forcing* to it.

TO COLOUR RAISIN WINES.

Wine made of raisins of the sun is always of the colour of rhenish, which is almost white. Very often that which is made of malaga's (especially if the fruit be but indifferent) will not hold its colour, but must have a colour laid on it.

The right colour of raisin wine is the colour of mountain. You must take care that your wine has not a great bottom in it; for if it has, 'twill be longer before it falls fine.

In order to lay a mountain colour on your wine, you must take three or four pounds of brown sugar, according to the quantity of wine you want to colour. Put it in an iron pan or iron ladle, set it over the fire, and keep stirring it about. Let it burn in this manner 'till it is quite black and bitter, which will be in about half an hour.

If you burn one pound of sugar, put a quart of boiling hot water to it; stir it about, and let it boil a quarter of an hour longer, then take it off and let it cool. A pint of this mixture is sufficient to colour a pipe of wine; but note, that with every pint you must mix a quarter of an ounce of common allum pounded to a fine powder; which will set the colour so that it will not subside, other wise it will fall to the bottom, and have no good effect on the liquor.

If you would have your wine of the colour of port, you must take eight ounces of logwood raspings, four ounces of alkanet root, one ounce of cochineal. Infuse them over a slow fire for three hours; strain the liquor from the wood, and keep it boiling. Then burn three pounds of brown sugar as before, and put the colour'd liquor to it; boil all together a quarter of an hour longer; then take it off, and when cold, bottle it for use.

A pint of this liquor will make a pipe the colour of port wine. You must always remember to set the colour with a quarter of an ounce of common allum, ground or beaten to a fine powder.

PART III.

THE HOUSEKEEPERS DIRECTOR.

FORCING FOR BEER.

There are two sorts of forcings for beer; for what will agree with one kind of beer will not serve for another. Some beer when kept twelve or fourteen months will taste as new and sweet as if not brew'd more than six or seven, nay a much shorter time, which must have a different forcing from that which is proper for beer that is ripe or less sweet.

Beers that are full and sweet must be forc'd in the following manner, viz.

For a hogshead, take a gallon of stale cyder, likewise one ounce of isinglass beat and pulled to small pieces, with an ounce of common allum ground to a fine powder, put them to the cyder; whisk it well together and let it stand 'till it's a jelly. Then break it in your can, and put one ounce of cream of tartar, and two pounds of stone-dust to it; whisk it well together, and dilute it with some of the beer till you have made the gallon five. Apply it to the hogshead, and stir it well about; and when the ferment is gone off (which will be in two or three hours) bung it up close. Leave out the vent-peg; and in a day or two you'll find it fine and bright.

Beers that are not Sweet are forced with *stum*, the same that is made for raisin wine, with this difference only, that you must take for one hogshead, three pints, and two pounds of alabaster; stir them well together, and dilute with beer as above. This will carry down all the foul particles, and make the beer fine in three or four hours.

* * * * *

FORCING FOR ALE.

ALE that is brew'd in the winter to be drank in about two months is apt to get foul, occasion'd by the brewer's neglecting it when cooling. Sometimes it is left out in the frost, which will chill it, and make it curdy as it were, and and foul; to remedy this you must

Take two gallons of cyder, and put two ounces of insinglass to it. When it is a jelly, add to them two pounds of brick-rubbings; whisk them well together, and dilute with some of the ale. Put the whole in the hogshead, and stir all about very well. When the ferment is a little off, bung it close; the next day give it vent, and you'll find it fine.

ALE OR BEER ACID.

If your beer or ale be a little prick'd, you must take for each hogshead a gallon of lac, boil it with an ounce of isinglass, drain it, and when cold, put to it two pounds of alabaster, two pounds of calcined chalk, and one ounce of salt of tartar. Stir them well together, and apply to the hogshead.

Mind that the cask be full, and this will immediately discharge the acid part from it, (as in page 12.) Bung it up for three or four days 'till it is settled; then rack it into a clean hogshead, and put two quarts of *ale forcing* to it, and bung it close.

BEER OR ALE ROPY, TO CURE.

If beer or ale should at any time get ropy, as in other disorders, you must proportion the strength of your remedy to the degree of the disorder. But beer or ale is seldom known to be so ropy as cyder.

Take, for one hogshead, two pounds of common allum in one lump, if possible; put it into a clear fire, and burn it an hour, then pound it, and apply to the hogshead. Stir it well for half an hour. This will cut the rope in a day or two; then rack it and force it with the same *stum forcing* at is directed for beer that is not sweet, as in page 26. If the rope be but thin, one pound of allum will be sufficient. Hyssop will cut a thin rope in ale, but this always gives it a bad taste.

TO MAKE YEST, TO FERMENT NEW BEER.

Many people that live at a distance from any town, are at a great loss, especially in the winter time, for yest to brew with; I shall therefore here give them directions to make an artificial yest that will answer the purpose altogether as well as the natural.

Take two quarts of small beer and one ounce of isinglass; boil them together five or six minutes; put it into a can or pail, and whisk it till it comes to the consistence of yest; let it stand an hour after, then put it to your wort in the same manner you were used to do the natural yest; this will be sufficient to ferment a hogshead.

THE END.

Lector House believes that a society develops through a two-fold approach of continuous learning and adaptation, which is derived from the study of classic literary works spread across the historic timeline of literature records. Therefore, we aim at reviving, repairing and redeveloping all those inaccessible or damaged but historically as well as culturally important literature across subjects so that the future generations may have an opportunity to study and learn from past works to embark upon a journey of creating a better future.

This book is a result of an effort made by Lector House towards making a contribution to the preservation and repair of original ancient works which might hold historical significance to the approach of continuous learning across subjects.

HAPPY READING & LEARNING!

LECTOR HOUSE LLP
E-MAIL: lectorpublishing@gmail.com